CW00517907

Where to watch Game
IN THE
KRUGER NATIONAL PARK

BY NIGEL DENNIS

SUNBIRD
PUBLISHING

First published 2000

2 4 6 8 10 9 7 5 3
Sunbird Publishing (Pty) Ltd
34 Sunset Avenue, Llandudno, Cape Town, South Africa

Registration number: 4850177827

Copyright © text: Nigel Dennis
Copyright © photographs: Nigel Dennis
Copyright © maps: Sunbird Publishing
Copyright © published edition: Sunbird Publishing

Publisher Dick Wilkins
Consultant   Marc McDonald
Editor Brenda Brickman
Designer Mandy McKay
Maps John Hall
Production manager Andrew de Kock
Reproduction by Unifoto (Pty) Ltd, Cape Town
Printed and bound by Tien Wah Press (Pte) Ltd, Singapore

All rights reserved. No part of this publication may be reproduced, stored in a retrieval system or transmitted, in any form or by any
means, electronic, mechanical, photocopying, recording or otherwise, without the prior written permission of the copyright owner(s).

ISBN 0 624 03885 8

CONTENTS

INTRODUCTION   4

CROCODILE BRIDGE   12

BERG-EN-DAL   14

PRETORIUSKOP   16

SKUKUZA   18

LOWER SABIE   22

SATARA AND ORPEN   26

OLIFANTS   30

LETABA   34

MOPANI   38

SHINGWEDZI   40

PUNDA MARIA   44

PHOTO TIPS   46

CHECKLIST   48

INTRODUCTION

Rooibosrant Dam near Bateleur Bushveld Camp in the Shingwedzi region is a prime spot to observe the Park's aquatic birds.

The Kruger National Park is considered to be one of the greatest game parks in the whole of Africa. In fact, few national parks in the world can offer visitors the same opportunity to view such a rich diversity of animal species. However, as game is never evenly distributed in the Park, there can be no guarantee of the sighting of any particular animal in any particular spot. This guide to game-viewing – a compilation of information supplied by section rangers and other Kruger staff, as well as my own observations – is intended to substantially increase prospects of viewing game in Kruger.

As a wildlife photographer, I have been a regular visitor to the Park over the past decade. As a result, I have driven some of the routes through Kruger a hundred times or more. It is my belief, based on experience, that, by following the general game-viewing hints offered here, and by concentrating on the prime routes indicated on the area maps provided in this book, game-viewing experiences will be significantly enhanced.

SEASONS AND CYCLES

Game movements and concentrations in the Kruger Park are greatly influenced by the availability of surface water. The Kruger Park experiences a dry season from May through to October. Although these winter months are generally considered the best for game-viewing, the timing of animal movements is dependent on the amount of rainfall that fell during the previous summer. After a very wet summer, movements to areas surrounding rivers and dams usually occur late in the winter, making September the most consistently rewarding viewing period. In times of drought, these animal concentrations around water can begin as early as May or June, with a game-viewing bonanza continuing through until the first spring rains.

While the winter season is the most productive in terms of the numbers of species sighted, the Kruger summer also has its special attractions. Impala lambs are born in November and December, and migrant birds also peak at this time. Even the late summer period, when long grass makes most game-viewing difficult, may be especially rewarding, particularly after an overnight shower. An early morning game drive under these conditions may well produce sightings of lion and leopard, as they are averse to walking in long, wet grass, and so prefer to use roads for hunting activity.

As a general rule, it is not a good idea to spend long hours alongside water holes in summer-rainfall months, as the numerous natural pans throughout the Park will hold water, and game will be well dispersed. It is, therefore, better to cover as much ground as possible.

Aside from the seasonal variation in rainfall, Kruger also undergoes cycles of wet and dry periods, lasting several years. Although numbers of most species increase during wet cycles, with abundant browsing and grazing opportunities, as well as surface water surpluses, the winter concentrations of game are less pronounced. On top of this, the long grass and thick bush that covers much of the Kruger make it difficult to spot game. Game-viewing is at its very best at the onset of a drought following several years of above-average rainfall. At this stage, game numbers have peaked and gather in areas surrounding the few remaining water sources. A prolonged drought, unfortunately, also guarantees a general decline in game numbers, although lion and other predators may temporarily thrive on easy pickings.

THE SUCCESSFUL GAME DRIVE

The unpredictability of game-viewing is probably what makes the experience so fascinating. That said, the most consistently productive times are early morning and late afternoon. Unfortunately, in the more popular camps, keen game-viewers will begin lining up at the gate (up

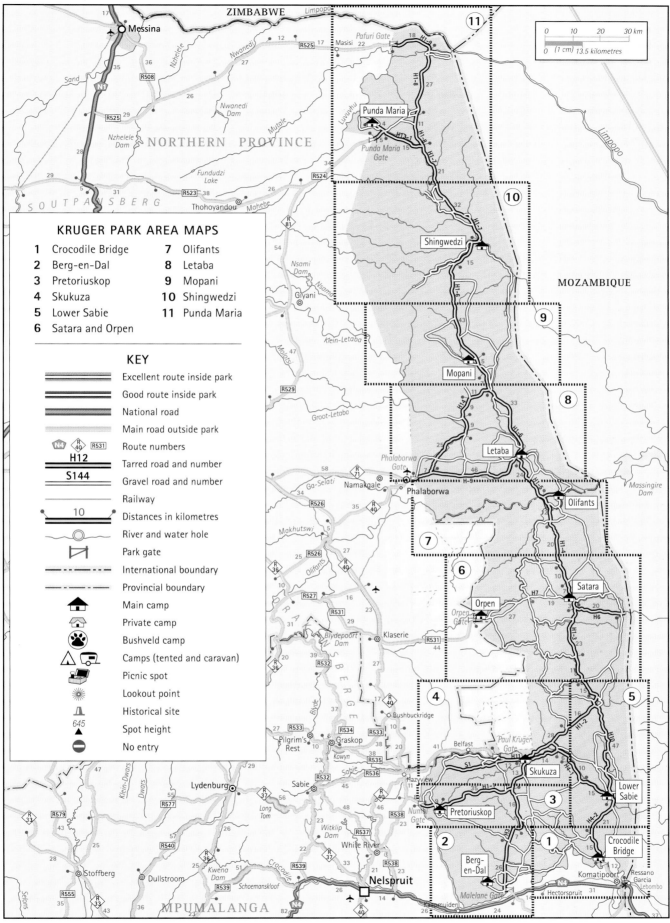

KRUGER PARK AREA MAPS

1 Crocodile Bridge   7 Olifants
2 Berg-en-Dal   8 Letaba
3 Pretoriuskop   9 Mopani
4 Skukuza   10 Shingwedzi
5 Lower Sabie   11 Punda Maria
6 Satara and Orpen

KEY

Excellent route inside park
Good route inside park
National road
Main road outside park
N4 R40 R531 Route numbers
H12 Tarred road and number
S144 Gravel road and number
Railway
10 Distances in kilometres
River and water hole
Park gate
International boundary
Provincial boundary
Main camp
Private camp
Bushveld camp
Camps (tented and caravan)
Picnic spot
Lookout point
Historical site
645 Spot height
No entry

to 30 cars at a time!), waiting impatiently for 'opening time' in the hope of being the first to view the morning's prime sightings. Personally, I prefer to wait until the early-bird entourage is a few kilometres down the road, and leave 10 minutes *after* the gates open.

In any event, big herds seldom appear around water holes until mid-morning. For this reason, I would recommend planning a steady, relaxed drive for the first three or four hours, followed by a break from about 9am alongside a water hole. At this stage, zebra, wildebeest, waterbuck, kudu, giraffe, and of course the ubiquitous impala, should be arriving in good numbers to drink.

Predator activity is slight during the midday period, when even the browsers and grazers prefer to seek shade. As this tends to be the least productive time of the day, it is probably wise to follow the animals' example and head for the shade. If you don't feel inclined to return to camp, picnic sites offer an opportunity to stretch your legs, and enjoy a leisurely lunch. Mid-afternoon, on the other hand, can yield excellent sightings at water holes. Along with the more common game species, elephant like to drink and bathe at this time of the day, and white rhino often put in an appearance in some areas.

As temperatures drop in the late afternoon, big cats, wild dog and hyena become active once again. The last couple of hours of daylight are best spent scanning the prime game-drive routes for these predators. It is worth staying out as late as possible, as the last half hour of daylight is prime leopard time. However, please ensure that you have sufficient time to return to camp before the gates close!

Temperature has a great influence on game activity. When temperatures soar into the forties much of the game activity is concentrated in brief periods very early and late in the day. At such times, it is wise to leave camp at the crack of dawn (gates open at 4.30am in mid-summer), and take a long siesta before venturing out again late in the afternoon.

Winter mornings, particularly in June and July, can be decidedly chilly, and the first hour after dawn may see little activity as, rather sensibly, the animals wait for the sun to warm the air a little. However, once out and about, game will continue to move until fairly late in the morning, and winter afternoons are frequently very productive. Cool, heavily overcast periods also significantly alter the pattern of activity. Even the big cats may continue hunting right through the day. In fact, cool, drizzly weather frequently produces leopard sightings, and these are just as likely to be at midday as any other time under these conditions.

HOW FAST SHOULD YOU DRIVE?

The Kruger National Park has strictly enforced speed limits: on tar the maximum is 50kph, and on gravel roads it is 40kph. To drive at the maximum speed means, however, that many of the best game sightings will surely be missed. In open country, I find viewing most rewarding at 25kph, and in thick, bushy areas, even 15kph may be too fast. Apart from the fact that game can be exceedingly difficult to spot in dense cover, safety is also a consideration. On many occasions I have turned a corner when driving through areas of dense mopane, only to find an elephant standing in the road. Had I been driving at the maximum speed limit, it would have been impossible to stop and the consequences disastrous!

THE BEST GAME-VIEWING VEHICLE

In high-rainfall years the grass in Kruger may reach a height of two metres or more. This can make game-viewing a very frustrating experience from the low vantage point of a sedan car. A minibus offers good height and excellent all-round visibility, and, while four-wheel drive is an unnecessary option because Kruger's roads are in excellent condition, these vehicles also have the advantage of height and big windows. For visitors hiring a vehicle to tour Kruger, I would recommend a Toyota Venture; while it is not a four-wheel-drive vehicle, it has all the advantages of one: height, big windows, and spaciousness, and the hire rates are considerably lower than for minibuses and four-wheel-drives. Note that only *enclosed* private vehicles are allowed in the Park, and that visitors may not alight vehicles except at designated sites.

Visitors receive a lesson in tracking and spoor on an South African National Parks-escorted day drive.

UP-TO-DATE INFO ON SIGHTINGS

Opportunities for consistently good game-viewing can be improved with a little current local knowledge. Most of the main camps have a 'sightings board', on which visitors are encouraged to place coloured pins on a map of the area to indicate interesting game sightings. All camps also have a 'sightings book', and it is worthwhile to check this too. Student rangers can be a mine of information; likewise, the staff at reception will have knowledge of the latest animal sightings. Of course, it can be also be helpful to compare notes with other visitors.

Many game sightings are fleeting, and it is futile to chase after a reported lone animal in the hope that it will stay in the area. However, animals with young seldom move far: a lone cheetah may cover considerable distances when hunting, but a cheetah mother with a small cub may stay in one area for several days. By the same token, a report of a pride of lion that has killed a small animal is unlikely to warrant a follow up. The prey will be consumed within minutes, and the pride will very likely have moved along rather rapidly. When lion bring down a big animal such as a giraffe or buffalo, where it usually takes a couple of days to consume the carcass, it is certainly worth following up. Reports of denning animals, particularly hyena and wild dog, are also opportunities for near-certain repeated sightings.

ESCORTED GAME DRIVES

South African National Parks (SANP) operate escorted drives in their own open vehicles.

Night drives have become particularly popular, offering opportunities to view the nocturnal creatures of the Park. The vehicles leave in the late afternoon and return to camp a couple of hours after dark. Of the smaller mammals, genet are frequently seen, and there is also a good chance of sighting civet, porcupine and white-tailed mongoose. Honey badger, aardvark and pangolin are also sometimes seen. Night drives offer the best possibilities of seeing black rhino, as well as other members of the Big Five.

Game tends to be scarce and skittish in windy conditions, so it is preferable to go on a night drive in calm, stable weather. Take along some warm clothing, as it can become very chilly on an open vehicle.

Escorted day drives, also in open SANP vehicles, are advantageous in that the staff conducting these drives have well-honed spotting skills and an intimate knowledge of the area, and some of the day drive routes utilise the 'no entry' patrol and firebreak roads, thus allowing entry

The hide at Bateleur often produces leopard sightings.

to areas not usually accessible to visitors. By the way, please don't be tempted to illegally traverse these no-entry roads. Apart from the fact that you will face a stiff fine if caught, there is a great risk of getting lost or stuck for several days. Some of the no-entry roads in this book have been marked as good/excellent routes, but please note that they are for the exclusive use of private/ bushveld camp guests.

A number of private operators also offer escorted tours in the south of the Park.

GAME-VIEWING FROM THE REST CAMPS

Some of Kruger's camps are situated near water holes, offering productive viewing on the camp's perimeter fence during the dry season. It is often worth taking a walk around the inside of the camp's perimeter fence. My only sighting of bushpig in Kruger was at Biyamiti Bush Camp, while taking just such a walk.

At Berg-en-Dal, I experienced one of the best leopard sightings I have had in my many years of visiting the Park. Surprisingly, it happened right in the middle of a warm afternoon – which just goes to show, you never can tell with this elusive spotted cat. A crowd gathered at the perimeter fence as a big male leopard hunted nearby, and we were treated to a 20-minute spectacle.

A night stroll along the perimeter fence, armed with a torch, will often reveal a nocturnal parade of genet and civet, and sometimes honey badger. Hyena, too, frequently patrol the camp fenceline after dark. Unfortunately this behaviour is probably the result of visitors feeding these animals scraps. I would urge visitors not to do this as it disrupts the animal's natural behaviour, and will result in a heavy fine if you are caught!

WHERE ARE THE LIONS?

I am sure that many of the Kruger reception staff wish they had been paid R10 for every time an eager visitor has asked this question! **Lion** are number one on the checklist for many of the Park's visitors. This is a pity as, for me, the great attraction of Kruger is its rich diversity of mammals, and not any single species.

My wife Wendy and I often chat to other visitors about their sightings, as we frequently learn of good photo opportunities. When we ask, 'what did you see this morning?' we have learned that if the reply is 'oh, nothing much,' it usually means that a great many species were seen – but no lion! Having tried to put 'lion mania' in perspective, I have to admit that these magnificent creatures also instill in me a feeling of awe. So, how do you go about seeing lots of lion in Kruger?

Lion occur widely throughout the Park. However, certain areas, especially those with a high prey density, produce a greater incidence of sightings. Also, larger prides often occur in these prime areas. In my experience, Satara provides the best base from which to look for lion. After that I would go for Lower Sabie/Crocodile Bridge, Skukuza, and Shingwedzi, in that order.

Although lion are often seen lying up in shade in the middle of the day, early and late game drives offer a much better opportunity to observe them on the hunt. My advice is to watch and listen carefully. If a herd of impala

This fully grown giraffe was brought down by a lone lioness.

is staring fixedly in one direction and snorting in alarm, it is a fairly sure sign that a predator is lurking. Likewise, baboon and vervet monkey will sound warnings from the tree tops at the approach of a lion. Giraffe behave rather strangely when they spot a lion: instead of running away, they often stare and then move a little closer for a better look! This might appear to be a death wish, but in fact they are likely to be at less risk if they know exactly where the lions are.

THE REST OF THE BIG FIVE

The magnificent **leopard** is my favorite African mammal, and I have spent a great deal of time searching for this wonderful but often elusive creature. Fortunately, it seems that the frequency of leopard sightings in the Park has increased over the past decade. I doubt that there are more leopards than before, but rather that, as result of a growth in tourist traffic, these animals have become relaxed in the presence of vehicles, and so are more likely to 'show' themselves.

Slow driving and careful scanning of the bush early and late in the day offer the best leopard-viewing opportunities. Search the trees as well as the ground, as leopard frequently carry their prey aloft to avoid the unwanted attention of lion and hyena, and may also climb onto a sturdy branch to have a quiet snooze.

Leopard have smaller territories than lion, and so recent sighting reports at the camps are good indicators of areas worth concentrating on. I must admit there is a considerable element of luck involved in finding leopard. During the five-month period I spent in Kruger in the winter of 1999, my total tally was a miserable three; and yet, one of the visitors with whom I spoke had seen no less than eight in one morning's drive!

Although both **black** and **white rhino** occur in fair numbers in the Park, the latter is by far the more commonly seen. In recent years, numbers of white rhino have increased considerably, and the Kruger population now stands at around 2 500 animals. Look for the telltale roadside dung middens. I have found the S3 gravel road that follows the Sabie River from Paul Kruger Gate to be the most consistently productive route for this animal. The last few kilometres before the S3 joins the S1 Doispane road can be especially rewarding, and I have seen as many as 10 white rhino on an afternoon drive on this route. The S1, which continues on through to Numbi Gate, is also an excellent rhino route. Generally, late afternoon produces the most white rhino sightings, although you may see them drinking and wallowing all day in warm, humid conditions.

The **black rhino** is an altogether different story. Firstly, at 250, the total population is one-tenth that of the white rhino. Black rhino are browsers, and so inhabit dense bush during the day, which makes them difficult to spot. The rarity of sightings, however, could be attributed to the fact that the Kruger population of these animals is shy and skittish. Unlike white rhino, which are usually unresponsive to vehicles, black rhino tend to bolt in fear at the sight of traffic. My feeling is that they purposefully keep away from roads during the daylight driving hours. You can consider yourself very fortunate to see a black rhino during the day from the tourist roads, and, generally, night drives offer a fairer opportunity to spot these magnificent creatures, as do escorted day walks.

Buffalo and **elephant** are easy to spot, and both occur in good numbers and are widely distributed throughout the Park. Latest counts indicate that Kruger is home to 21 000 buffalo, and some 8 800 elephant.

Hot spots for sighting big elephant herds include the Lower Sabie and Crocodile Bridge areas, Satara, Letaba, Mopani, and especially Shingwedzi in the Kanniedood region. Large buffalo herds may also be seen in many areas. As with elephant, I have found the S50 gravel road that skirts Kanniedood Dam and the Shingwedzi River to be a prime area. The general area within 20 kilometres of Shingwedzi Camp, along with Letaba, Satara, Skukuza and Lower Sabie, all offer a good chance of seeing impressively large buffalo herds.

OTHER PREDATORS

Among the other large predators, **spotted hyena** are the most numerous and frequently seen in the Park. These animals often use roadside culverts as dens, and both adults and pups are accepting of vehicle presence. Roadside dens offer fantastic game-viewing opportunities, so it is well worth inquiring as to their whereabouts. Hyena pups show great curiosity and will often take a playful exploratory nip at a car bumper! Apart from the den sites, spotted hyena are regularly encountered throughout the Park. As is to be expected with a nocturnal predator, the best time to see these animals is early and late in the day, and, of course, on night drives.

The Kruger National Park is an important stronghold for the highly endangered **wild dog**. The population fluctuates from time to time, and at present has dipped just below 400 animals. Wild dog are wanderers, which

A young hyena photographed at a roadside den a few kilometres from Shingwedzi Camp.

accounts for surprisingly regular sightings, considering their rather modest numbers and the vastness of Kruger. They also favour hunting from roads, and a pack will often rest up at the roadside. During much of the year, it is almost impossible to predict where a wild dog pack will appear. It is usually only during the June to September denning season that sightings occur regularly in a specific area. Young pups are not strong enough to accompany the hunting adults, so the pack concentrates activities within range of the den. Regular reports of sightings in a particular area during the winter months usually indicate that the dogs are denning close by. Occasionally, wild dog too will den in a roadside culvert. I had the privilege of seeing a roadside den close to Pretoriuskop Camp a few years ago. The regular wild dog activity often caused a considerable traffic jam, with the tiny black puppies wandering among the cars. It is a wonder that none were run over!

Diurnal predators, **cheetah** occur in small numbers, and can be extremely elusive. Lion, hyena and leopard all 'pirate' prey killed by cheetah. This, as well as a high rate of infant mortality (also caused by other predators), keeps numbers rather low. In fact, the entire cheetah population of Kruger is thought to be only in the region of 200 animals. Most of my cheetah sightings have been on open plains that tend to have a lower density of lion. For many years, Lower Sabie has been the most consistently rewarding cheetah spot, particularly in the Duke water hole region, and along the H10 tar road north, towards Mlondozi. Cheetah often hunt later in the day than lion

Vervet monkey are particularly common in the riverine areas, and offer fascinating viewing opportunities.

and leopard, so even if you do not manage to spot one in the first few hours of the day, persistence may pay off.

Among the smaller predators, the **black-backed jackal** is most frequently seen. The black-backed jackal will often follow and mob leopard, and to recognise this mobbing call would mean easy location of leopard. They also scavenge and attempt to grab tidbits at the kills of larger predators. The **side-striped jackal** is also present, however, it tends to be predominantly nocturnal, and is certainly far shyer. All my side-striped sightings have been very early or late in the day, on quiet back roads. Even so, these wary animals have always run from my approaching vehicle, and in all the time I have spent in the Park I have yet to obtain a worthwhile photograph of one!

Caracal and **serval** are also very shy creatures, and are rarely seen. Both probably exist in greater numbers than is realised, but any sightings can indeed be considered to be a game-watcher's red-letter day. In the case of serval, my two brief sightings have both been in marshy habitat that is typical of this species.

THE PRIMATES

Both **chacma baboon** and **vervet monkey** are so frequently encountered in Kruger that many visitors scarcely give them a second glance. This is a pity as both species can offer delightful and very entertaining viewing. The large baboon troops with many youngsters can be particularly interesting, and present superb opportunities for photography. I find there is usually so much happening that I can easily shoot roll after roll of film.

THE BROWSERS

Giraffe are particularly common in the central and southern regions, and densities here are among the highest found anywhere on the continent. **Kudu** is another common browser. These impressive, large animals are easy to spot.

Nyala, once found mainly in the Pafuri region, can now be seen as far south as the Sabie River, and are regularly encountered along the very popular H4-1 Skukuza to Lower Sabie route. The H4-1 is also one of the best places to see **bushbuck**.

Also a browser, the **klipspringer** frequents rocky outcrops virtually throughout the Park.

THE GRAZERS

Hippo are widely distributed and may be found in all of the larger rivers and dams. The Kruger population stands at over 2 900. They leave their watery sanctuary at night to graze in the adjacent riverine areas, although during long, dry periods hippo may be forced to travel some distance in search of suitable fodder. A field ranger is on duty at the Hippo Pool on the S27, close to Crocodile Bridge, to escort visitors on the short walk to a large pool in the Crocodile River. The hippo here are accustomed to human presence on the bank, permitting excellent viewing and photography. The sizeable Sirheni Dam at Sirheni Bushveld Camp skirts the camp's perimeter fence, ensuring good, close-up views, especially at night, when hippos graze right up to the fence.

'Plains game' – **zebra** and **wildebeest** – are found throughout Kruger. Very large herds gather for winter grazing in the Muntshe area to the north of Lower Sabie. At times, many hundreds of these animals can be seen from the H10 road.

Waterbuck, as the name suggests, are found in association with water. About 1 500 exist in the Park, and during dry spells concentrations are found close to the remaining water sources.

The rapier horns and muscular appearance of the **sable** make this one of Kruger's most impressive antelope. Small herds are widely scattered, but the H1-2 north of Skukuza in the Mantimahle Dam area, and the nearby S36 route up to Manzimhlope Windmill, both produce regular sightings of the rare sable.

The **eland** is the largest antelope in Kruger, but most herds are skittish and wary of approaching vehicles, and sightings are irregular. Most of my eland sightings have been on the H1-7 tar road to the north of Shingwedzi.

Tsessebe are also present, but again only in small numbers, mainly in the central and northern areas.

Roan are susceptible to drought, and have become exceedingly rare in recent years. Hopefully, the breeding project in a huge enclosure north of Babalala will produce enough of these beautiful creatures to replenish the tiny remaining population in Kruger.

Lichtenstein's hartebeest became extinct in Kruger around the turn of the century. This animal is common in the central African highlands, and some years ago a number of animals from the Kasungu National Park in Malawi were reintroduced. Currently, it is thought that there are about 45 of these beasts in the Park. Sightings occur very rarely.

SMALL GAME

A number of **mongoose** species are present in Kruger. Most frequently encountered are the dwarf, banded and slender varieties. The slender mongoose is often seen crossing a road, but dives for cover at the approach of a vehicle. A social species, the **banded mongoose** lives in packs of up to 30 individuals. The pack moves very quickly on foraging expeditions, ensuring little more than a glimpse of this creature. Of the three species, the **dwarf mongoose** provides the best opportunities for viewing and photography. Often found living in termite mounds, the dwarf mongoose, like the banded, is also a social species. Early morning and again late in the afternoon, the adults in the group gather at their termite-mound home to groom, while the young play nearby. These delightful little mongooses provide wonderful viewing, and in terms of their tameness and easily observable social interaction, are the closest thing in Kruger to the wonderful meerkats or suricates of the Kalahari.

In many game reserves, **steenbok** and **common duiker**, in particular, are very shy, secretive creatures, and are difficult to observe. The high volume of traffic in Kruger has meant that these animals have become so habituated that they hardly bother to glance up when a car passes by. This is particularly evident in the Skukuza area.

Similar in appearance to the steenbok is the less common **Sharpe's grysbok**. It is useful to carry a mammal field guide to note the subtle differences between the two. Sharpe's grysbok is most likely to be seen in the northern areas. For many years a hot spot for these creatures has been the northern part of the Red Rocks Loop near Shingwedzi. In just the last year or so they have also been seen regularly from the tar road leading north from

Ever alert for predators, a large herd of impala drinks at a water hole close to Lower Sabie.

Shingwedzi Camp. A friend told me recently that the grysbok he saw there was so close to the road that he found it difficult to obtain a satisfactory photograph!

Most of the remainder of Kruger's **small mammals** are primarily nocturnal. These species include **civet, genet, honey badger, porcupine, African wildcat, bushpig, pangolin, white-tailed mongoose** and **bushbaby**. As I mentioned earlier, the best time to see these creatures is on a night drive, or a night-time stroll around the camp's perimeter fence. However, bushbaby occur inside many of the rest camps – listen for their nocturnal calls and search the adjacent trees with a torch. Also, genet and sometimes even civet enter many of the camps late at night – probably looking for braai scraps.

A dwarf mongoose at its termite-mound home in the far north of the Kruger National Park.

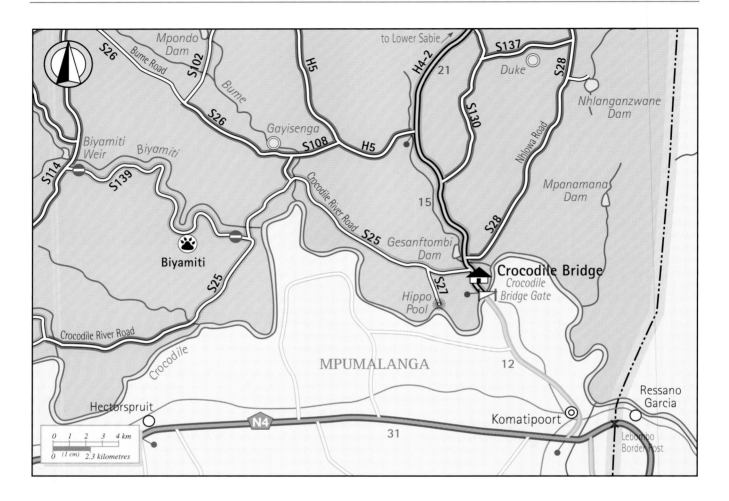

The Crocodile Bridge area is probably one of the most underrated in the entire Park. I have had consistently good sightings here. However, it was only when I started to assess the routes in the region for this guide that I realised that almost every road warranted either a good or excellent rating! As well as having a high density of general game, there is an excellent chance of seeing all of the Big Five in this area.

The camp itself is a delightful spot, green and well shaded. Crocodile Bridge is a fairly small camp, and as such does not have its own restaurant, but the shop at camp reception is well stocked. The camp also serves as an entrance gate, so there can be a considerable amount of through traffic during school holidays.

Only a couple of kilometres north of Crocodile Bridge on the H4-2, the **Gesanftombi Dam** attracts large numbers of game. By mid-morning there are usually herds of zebra, wildebeest and impala milling around, along with plenty of

giraffe. Many rate the H4-2 tar road through to Lower Sabie as one of the most productive in the entire Park.

Elephant, white rhino and lion are frequently seen, and wild dog sightings are reported regularly. The H4-2 is a busy route for through traffic travelling north, so it is a good idea to travel along this road in the early hours of the day, and to traverse one of the gravel roads on your return trip to camp. The S28 Nhlowa road is a good choice, as there is a fair chance of seeing cheetah and white rhino along this road, as well as plenty of other game.

The S25 Crocodile River road is another prime route. Leopard are likely to be seen along this road in the early morning and late afternoon, and lion are very plentiful along the entire route. A few kilometres from the camp along the S25, a short track (S27) branches to the left, leading to a **Hippo Pool**. Here a field ranger is on duty daily to escort visitors on the short walk to view the hippos close-up. If you are traversing the S25 in the mid-afternoon, a short detour to **Gayisenga water hole** on the S26 is likely to yield elephant. This water hole attracts plenty of game, and is, in fact, a pool on the **Mpondo Spruit**, which is generally dry throughout much of its course.

Although the immediate area around Crocodile Bridge often teems with game, the camp makes a good base from which to make longer trips to other excellent areas.

The route through and beyond Lower Sabie is very productive, as is the **Mpondo Dam** area on the S102.

Biyamiti Bushveld Camp is situated about 25 kilometres west of Crocodile Bridge. In recent years, Biyamiti has become very popular with visitors, and rightly so as the area offers outstanding game-viewing. The 22-kilometre S139 is accessible only to visitors staying at Biyamiti. This is one of the most productive roads in the Park for leopard, and there is a very good chance of seeing the rest of the Big Five as well. Even in the wet summer months, when viewing is patchy in many areas, the S139 remains consistently productive. Word seems to have spread regarding the excellent game-viewing at Biyamiti, and it is advisable to book several months in advance to be ensure accommodation here.

Lion are frequently seen on the S25 Crocodile Bridge road.

The S28, and particularly the S137 in the vicinity of Duke water hole, regularly produce sightings of cheetah.

BERG-EN-DAL

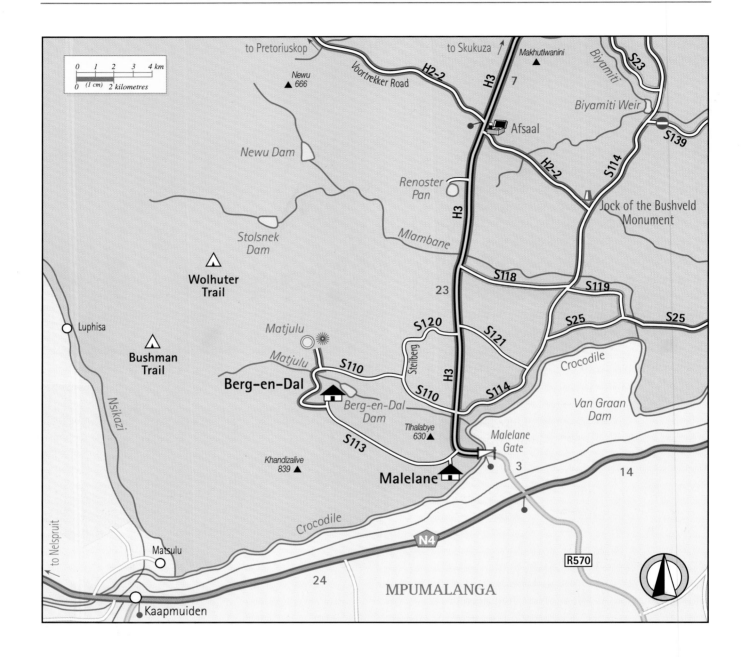

B erg-en-Dal is Kruger's only camp that is set in rugged mountain scenery. Attractive, modern chalets and a large, shady camp site make this an agreeable place to stay. A dam adjacent to the camp provides worthwhile viewing, and bird life in the camp itself is prolific. During the winter, aloe-flowering season, sunbirds gather here in great numbers. The rocky Malelane mountains offer spectacular views of the surrounding area and, following good rains, wild flowers abound. It is often necessary to do a fair amount of driving in order to find game, as densities are fairly low in this area. Close to camp, the four-kilometre route to the **Matjulu water hole** is sometimes rewarding. Rhino drink here most evenings, and leopard are seen from time to time. Giraffe and kudu are often in the vicinity, although not in great numbers.

The S110 gravel road continues on past Matjulu for six kilometres, but offers rather patchy viewing. From here you could continue along the S110 for a further four kilometres before joining the main H3 route, or follow

Rocky outcrops – known as koppies *– are typical of the Berg-en-Dal region.*

Covered by red-billed oxpeckers, a pair of female kudu enjoy a mid-morning drink.

the winding S120 Steilberg route. Although I have had very good white rhino sightings in this area, game along this route is generally sparse.

The H3 tar road from Malelane to Skukuza carries heavy traffic, but can offer surprisingly worthwhile game-viewing. Cheetah are common along this road, and hyena regularly use roadside culverts to den. As always, it pays to drive slowly; hyena pups often sit only metres from the roadside, and it is very easy to sail right past without noticing them. Two kilometres off the H3 on a dirt track, lies **Renoster Pan** (Rhino Pan). I must admit I have yet to see rhino drinking here, but this water hole draws fair numbers of general game.

Continuing north on the H3 past the **Afsaal picnic site** is the steep and rocky **Makhutlwanini** mountain. This area is prime klipspringer habitat, and opportunities of spotting this remarkably agile little antelope here are excellent.

Probably the most rewarding game area in the Berg-en-Dal region lies to the east of the H3. Between Malelane Gate and Afsaal, a total of four gravel roads branch off into this area. This is good lion, leopard, hyena and white rhino country. My favourite is the southernmost route, the S114, which skirts the Crocodile River and the southern boundary of the Kruger Park. Unfortunately, a great deal of unsightly building development has taken place on private land on the opposite bank of the river. However, the bounty of game to be seen along this route – particularly waterbuck and white rhino – does compensate.

After eight kilometres, the S114 joins the S25, running right the way through to Crocodile Bridge. The entire route is excellent for lion, and I have often spotted several prides in a morning's drive.

The S119, which branches off to the left, is a short but fascinating back road. This road closely follows the **Mlambane Spruit**, and a number of interesting loops branch off the S119, offering excellent access and fabulous viewing.

Look out for a small seasonal pan set among thick trees and bushes. Good numbers of game drink here, and I rate this as the best water hole in the Park at which to photograph white rhino.

Unlike so many water holes in Kruger, this pan is ideally situated for photography, and only requires a moderate telephoto lens for good portraits of rhino drinking and wallowing.

Formerly a private camp, *Malelane* (near Berg-en-Dal) is now open to the general public, and offers reasonably priced rondavels and a limited number of camp sites. Although situated only four kilometres from Malelane Gate, this looks to be an attractive and peaceful spot.

The seasonal pan on the S119 is much favoured by the stout, square-lipped white rhino, and offers good photo opportunities.

PRETORIUSKOP

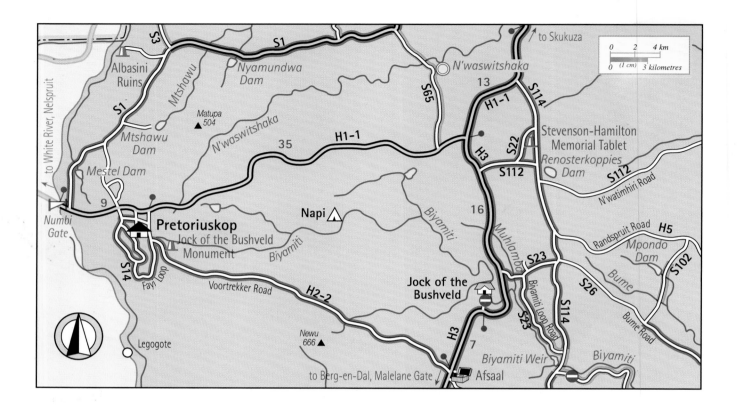

Pretoriuskop is the third-largest camp in the Park. It is also one of the highest, coolest and wettest areas in Kruger. The latter results in tall grass and thick bush, making game-viewing difficult: during the high rainfall years the grass cover can reach heights of over two metres! However there is a good game population, and I have had some very worthwhile sightings during long, dry spells, when much of the grass cover has been eaten or flattened.

The surrounding area holds plenty of white rhino, buffalo and kudu. Predators are well represented, with regular sightings of lion and leopard.

Immediately west of the camp several roads wind through an attractive area of rocky outcrops and *koppies*. Leopard are seen here from time to time, although, apart from the odd kudu, baboon troops, and small herds of impala, I have not had much luck on this route. However, it is a pleasant scenic drive, and very popular with visitors staying at Pretoriuskop. After exploring the loop roads, it is good idea to head off on the H2-2 Voortrekker road. Wild dog and cheetah are sometimes in the area, although in the case of wild dog, sightings are unpredictable.

Another productive route to take is the main H1-1 road that leads to Numbi Gate, and turn right along the S1. I have seen plenty of lion and white rhino along this route, and the large **Mestel Dam** attracts general game.

A longer, but worthwhile drive would involve continuing on the S1 and onto the S3. This area can be exceptionally fruitful if you are looking for the Big Five, and is described in detail in the Skukuza section.

I have also included in this area, the eastern Renosterkoppies and Mpondo dam regions. Even though these areas are closer to Skukuza, they are easily accessible from Pretoriuskop via the H1-1 Napi road.

While I have seldom seen large numbers of game on the H1-1, I have over the years been pleasantly surprised by sightings of wild dog and cheetah, and have had a splendid mid-morning eyeful of a leopard on the hunt.

Renosterkoppies Dam is reached by taking either the S112 or the S22 that bypasses the **Stevenson Hamilton Memorial Tablet**. I find the latter to be the more interesting and productive of the two routes. There are some good rocky outcrops – complete with klipspringer – along the way, and kudu are usually plentiful. Hyena are also often seen at a den site here. Renosterkoppies is appropriately named, as white rhino regularly drink here. This is one of several water holes in Kruger where the animals seem to enjoy standing around after drinking, and as a rule, good numbers of wildebeest, zebra and warthog are also present.

The S114 south of Renosterkoppies, although not the prettiest of drives, regularly offers sightings of lion and leopard. A worthwhile detour from here would be to visit **Mpondo Dam**; take the H5 Randspruit road off the S114 to the dam. Rejoin the S114 by taking the S26 Bume road. Mpondo is a very large dam, so game tends to be too distant to photograph, but the sheer numbers of animals that gather here present an impressive spectacle.

I recommend that you follow the S114 right the way through to Biyamiti Weir. This is a wonderful spot to watch and photograph water birds at very close range. Klipspringer inhabit the surrounding koppies and leopard sightings are frequently reported. Just to the north of Biyamiti Weir, the S23 Biyamiti Loop road branches off to the left. Following the Muhlamba Spruit, elephant herds and good numbers of giraffe are often present along this attractive riverine route.

The handsome brown-hooded kingfisher – actually a nonaquatic bird – is a common resident throughout the Park.

Blue wildebeest prefer to graze on short, nutritious grass. Numbers may decline in high rainfall cycles, when tall, rank grass predominates.

SKUKUZA

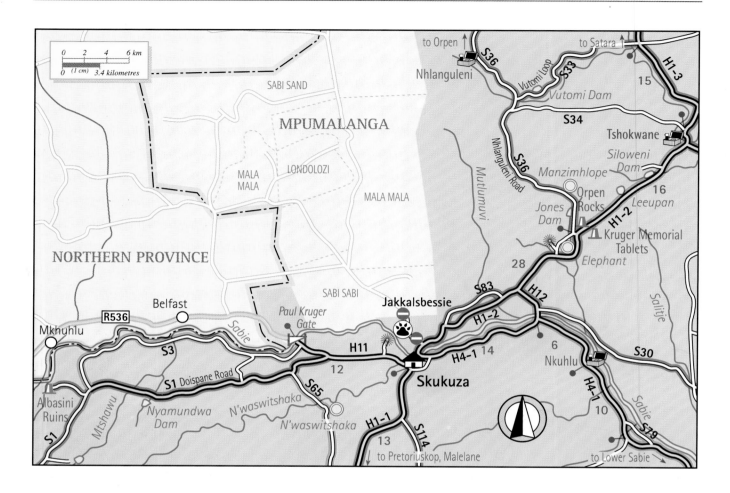

S kukuza is by far the largest camp in the Kruger National Park. With over 200 huts, a huge camping area complete with shops, restaurant, movie theatre, doctors' rooms, a petrol station, etc., it resembles a small town rather than a rest camp!

Some enormous specimens of crocodile inhabit the Sabie River, and are easily viewed from the numerous loop roads on the H4-1.

Although the main tar roads in the vicinity are invariably busy, many of the gravel roads can offer surprisingly private viewing.

A great variety of game may be seen in the area from all of the many excellent routes, and several roads in the Skukuza area are among the most productive in the Park. With so many possible routes, Skukuza warrants a fairly long stay in order to explore the area properly. Having said that, it is probably wise to avoid this busy camp during peak holiday times.

The H4-1 tar road that follows the **Sabie River** is a very popular route. Magnificent fig trees line the banks, making this a scenic drive as well as an exceptionally productive game-viewing drive. Often, there is so much to see that I find it takes me several hours simply to drive the first dozen kilometres.

It is a good idea to explore the many loop roads along the way as they offer good views of the river. Hippo are numerous here, and huge crocodile live in the river too.

Keen bird-watchers should keep a lookout for the rare and elusive African finfoot, which is found here.

Riverine bush alongside the Sabie is home to many leopard, and lion are likely to be seen hunting in the area. In fact, you could well see just about everything along this route – elephant, giraffe, hyena, as well as some of the largest baboon troops to be found anywhere in the Park. Although the constant flow of traffic can be annoying, the H4-1 is also a prime route for photographers. The animals in the area are so used to the presence of vehicles that very close views are possible, and this is one of the easiest places to photograph normally shy, skittish species, such as bushbuck, steenbok and duiker.

While the H4-1 remains productive all the way through to Lower Sabie, I often prefer to turn left off of the H4-1 and onto the H12, crossing a picturesque, fast flowing stretch of the Sabie River. Immediately over the river bridge the S30 Salitje road branches off to the right. The first five kilometres of this route are exceptional, as game is prolific, with a high frequency of lion sightings.

Oblivious to road traffic, a steenbok feeds alongside the busy H4-1.

The S30 Salitje road is an excellent game route. Seasonal pans alongside this route attract many species, including zebra herds.

The rare and regal-looking sable is fairly frequently seen near Manzimhlope water hole on the S36.

Numerous loop roads radiate from the S30, all of them with pretty river views. The S30 continues for some 18 kilometres, but once the road leaves the Sabie River, game usually becomes less plentiful.

I prefer to take the H1-2 back to Skukuza, rather than repeating a journey along the H4-1. The low-level bridge where the H1-2 crosses the **Sand River** is a hot spot for lion and leopard sightings.

An interesting, albeit longer drive involves continuing north on the H1-2 to **Elephant water hole**. This attractive spot is clearly sign-posted, and a short gravel track leads to the water point. Despite its name, elephants are not always present, but plenty of general game can usually be seen.

A short distance north of here, the S36 Nhlanguleni gravel road branches off to the left. Sable are very likely to be seen in this area. A third water hole – **Manzimhlope** – on the S36, is a good spot for these rare animals, and is also noted as a **prime photographic venue**. The natural-looking pan fed by a wind pump is situated right next to the road on the left-hand side, and the setting is **perfect for morning photography**.

Beyond Manzimhlope, the S36 is sometimes a little slow for game sightings, but it is worth persevering in order to reach the S33 Vutomi Loop. This 19-kilometre gravel road consistently offers lion sightings, and the **Vutomi Dam** along the way is a good place to photograph giraffe as they assume their awkward stance to drink water from the dam.

To return to Skukuza Camp, take the H1-3 road that leads towards Tshokwane, and then the main H1-2 road to Skukuza. It is worth making a quick stop at **Siloweni**

In the winter dry season, large buffalo herds congregate alongside the Sabie River and surrounding areas.

The Skukuza region supports a prolific leopard population. Mostly solitary by nature, these magnificent predators favour both riverine bush and rocky areas.

Dam and **Leeupan** (Lion Pan) on the way back, as both water holes draw good numbers of game.

Visitors who wish to avoid the hoards of cars normally associated with Skukuza would do well to try the areas to the west of the camp. The many excellent viewing roads in this region are less frequently travelled.

Head towards the **Paul Kruger Gate** and turn left onto the S3 gravel road. This normally quiet road that runs alongside the Sabie River is a prime route, and is consistently productive for elephant, lion and leopard. The last few kilometres of the S3 are among the best places to see white rhino in the entire Park.

I usually follow the S1 Doispane road to return to Skukuza. Although game is not prolific along this road, it often offers the opportunity to view wild dog, and I have also had luck with leopard sightings here.

It is sometimes worthwhile to leave the S1 briefly to investigate the S65. This road rarely carries much traffic, although in recent years it has become known as a prime area for leopard. Also on the S65 is the **N'waswitshaka water hole**. It is a pity that so many of the water holes and windmills in the Kruger Park are poorly situated for

photography. Often the water hole, and so the game that come to drink from it, is simply too far from the road, or vegetation obscures the view; sometimes even the light direction is wrong. Fortunately, the natural-looking pan at N'waswitshaka is very close to the road, and is ideally situated for afternoon photography.

The prolific H4-1 route offers a variety of sightings, which may include the stately nyala.

LOWER SABIE

Lower Sabie enjoys a well-deserved reputation of being an outstanding area from which to view game, and, as a result, the camp has a very high occupancy rate. In fact, it is wise to **book in advance**, especially if you intend to visit during the popular winter period. The camp itself is lushly green and pleasant, and has a wonderful variety of 'resident' bird species. Unfortunately, because of its location alongside the **Sabie River**, this camp has for many years had a high incidence of malaria cases. This should not serve as a deterrent to visiting Lower Sabie, but it is essential to use precautions such as insect repellents, to avoid being bitten by mosquitoes, and to take the necessary antimalarial medication, or prophylactics.

Any one of the three main viewing routes that radiate from the camp will offer varied and productive viewing, so it can be a tough decision knowing which one to explore first! One of my favourites is the main H4-2 heading south towards Crocodile Bridge. Lion, leopard and elephant are common along this entire road. Some fine herds of buffalo are also present, and are usually encountered in the first eight or so kilometres, where the H4-2 runs quite close to the Sabie River. White rhino too occasionally occur along this road, as do sizeable herds

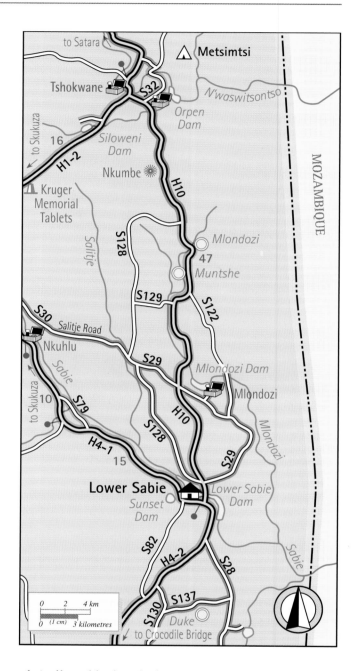

Lower Sabie is prime Big Five country. Elephant, which number some 8 800 in total in the Kruger National Park, are particularly common, especially along the H4-2 route.

of giraffe and kudu. The best reward I have had over the last few years while travelling along the H4-2 has been the regular sighting of wild dog. Overall, this must be one of the top roads in the Park for both numbers and diversity of game.

Although the H4-2 is consistently productive all the way through to Crocodile Bridge, it is often worth the effort to traverse the gravel roads to the east of this route. The bush here is rather flat and featureless, but interesting game sightings compensate to a large degree.

The riverine areas close to Lower Sabie are ideal waterbuck habitat. Here a family of these elegant antelope, with their white-ringed rumps, is alert to the ever-present danger of predation by lion.

Both the S28 and the S137, leading to **Duke water hole**, offer a fair opportunity to see cheetah and wild dog. A large pride of lion is also regularly seen in the vicinity of Duke, along with plenty of giraffe.

If you head west on the S137 past Duke and turn right onto the S130, a small natural pan lies on the left-hand side, a short distance along this road. On every occasion that I have travelled this route towards evening, I have come across white rhino drinking at the pan. The rhino seem to favour this spot at dusk, and, fortunately, it is a fairly short 15-kilometre drive back to Lower Sabie from here, so it is possible to see the rhinos and get back to camp before the gates close.

The H4-1 main route through to Skukuza is both productive and very popular.

Sunset Dam lies to the left, barely a kilometre from Lower Sabie. This is a favourite venue of photographers, and is particularly notable for the variety of water birds within easy camera range. Yellow-billed and marabou stork

Yellow-billed stork, along with many other aquatic bird species, may be viewed at Sunset Dam.

Winter grazing along the H10 attracts the largest concentration of plains game in the entire Park.

are nearly always present, and sometimes saddle-billed and open-billed storks as well. Giant and pied kingfisher hunt from perches right next to the parking area, oblivious to vehicular traffic.

There are good numbers of hippo, and large herds of game drink throughout the day, including a group of fairly habituated waterbuck.

It is tempting to spend an entire morning at Sunset Dam, but with so much to see along the length of the H4-1, I generally move on after an hour or so.

Closely following the Sabie River, the H4-1 is a prime route for elephant, buffalo, and giraffe, as well as all of the common antelope species that occur in the Park. Of course, these regular game movements are a magnet for lion, and it is by no means unusual to spot several prides in a morning's drive. A short detour along the S79 gravel road is also very productive for buffalo and lion.

During the dry winter months, the region to the north of Lower Sabie provides one of the grand spectacles of the Kruger Park. At times, huge herds of zebra and wildebeest gather for winter grazing, and good numbers of elephant are often present as well.

The most productive area lies towards **Muntshe**, between 10 and 25 kilometres north of Lower Sabie on the H10. The big cats take advantage of such a high concentration of prey species, and on one memorable drive I saw cheetah, leopard and lion within the space of a few kilometres along this route. It is also worth driving down the back roads on either side of the H10, and there is a stunning view of **Mlondozi Dam** from the parking area off the S29.

Continuing north on the H10, the road leaves the plains and rises sharply to follow a rocky ridge. As is to be expected, there are plenty of klipspringer in this area. However, the presence of general game species is rather sparse. For those with an interest in botany, a rare succulent – the Lebombo euphorbia – grows profusely in this region.

The high vantage point of **Nkumbe Lookout** offers a grand vista of the seemingly endless bushveld below, and many consider this to be the most memorable scenic view in the Kruger Park.

About 13 kilometres north of Nkumbe, a quiet gravel road branches to the right. The S32 first skirts **Orpen Dam**, also offering an area in which to park and enjoy the fine view.

From here, the S32 twists and turns, closely following the **N'waswitsontso Spruit**. This is, to my mind, one of the great 'secret' roads in Kruger. Although very close to the busy **Tshokwane picnic area** on the main tar route, the S32 is seldom travelled, making it an attractive detour. This short drive through mature riverine vegetation boasts a notable variety of game. Giraffe and waterbuck abound, and it is a safe bet that concentrated searching must offer a chance of spotting a leopard.

It was here on an early morning drive that I had my best opportunity in many years to photograph the elusive, nocturnal serval.

In summer, white-fronted bee-eaters breed close to the H4-1, a few kilometres west of Lower Sabie.

A pair of young impala rams spar during the winter rutting season.

SATARA AND ORPEN

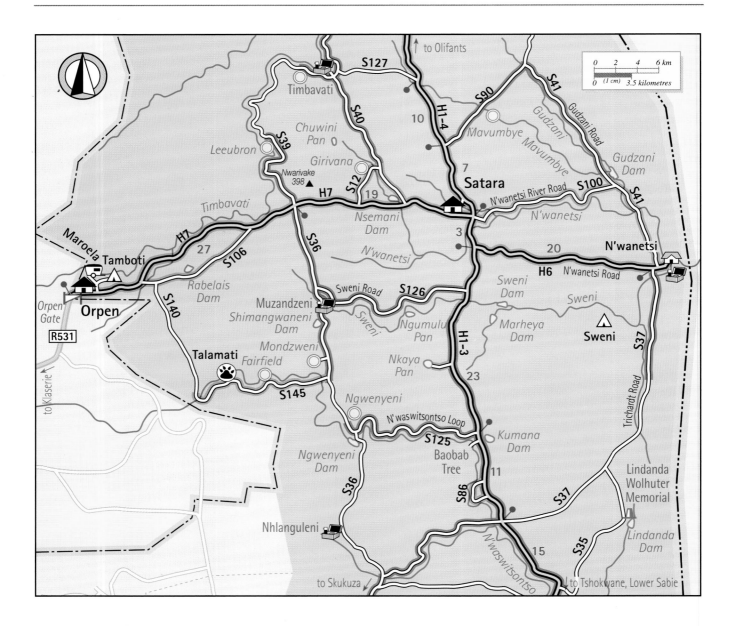

Satara has long enjoyed a dedicated following among regular visitors to Kruger. The plains surrounding the camp teem with game, and even within sight of the camp itself it is not unusual to see herds of zebra, wildebeest and waterbuck, as well as a sprinkling of giraffe and warthog. There are also plenty of elephant in the region, but it is the **frequency of lion sightings** that makes Satara the number-one option for so many regulars. This busy camp is second in size only to Skukuza. Fortunately, there are so many excellent routes radiating from Satara that, even during peak times, it is possible to find some quiet spots for game-viewing.

You needn't even leave camp to observe the wildlife, as a small water hole just beyond Satara's perimeter attracts a steady flow of thirsty game.

The S100 N'wanetsi River road is the most renowned viewing route close to Satara. I have heard of visitors having quite phenomenal game-viewing success here – upwards of 30 lion, as well as elephant and buffalo herds all in an hour or so of driving. Leopard sightings are often reported as well. I must admit that, although I have driven the S100 dozens and dozens of times, I have never had exceptional sightings: I guess it is just the luck of the draw!

At the end of the S100, visitors have the option of heading north along the S41 Gudzani road, or taking the southern route towards **N'wanetsi Private Camp**. Both routes are productive, but I generally find the southern route to be more so. From N'wanetsi there is an easy but also usually fruitful drive back to camp along the H6 tar road. It is possible to head south again on the S37 Trichardt road; the turnoff is a few kilometres onto the H6. You will have to allow plenty of time to look out for game along this road, as the route traverses almost 60 kilometres of the eastern plains before joining the main H1-3 from Skukuza to Satara. From this point, it is still a long drive back to Satara camp! In my experience, only the first dozen kilometres of the Trichardt road are productive, so unless you wish to make a very long drive exploring remote back roads, it is better to turn around after a short while and head back to the H6.

The area to the south of Satara also features several interesting and productive areas. The first 10 kilometres of the main H1-3 route heading towards Skukuza often produces sightings of lion, leopard, and plenty of giraffe.

Although the H1-3 can provide reasonable viewing right the way through to Tshokwane, I much prefer to turn off onto the S126 Sweni road, which carries far less traffic, and is a consistently productive route, and so warrants a slow drive in order to search the area thoroughly. This very pretty road usually offers a great variety of game, as well as the opportunity to see large prides of lion. A couple of years ago, I even had a very good sighting of caracal here – an animal seldom seen in the Kruger Park.

After 22 kilometres, you will arrive at the **Muzandzeni picnic area,** and join the S36. After travelling in a southerly direction for 11 kilometres along the S36, you will reach the **Mondzweni water hole.** Lion favour this area, and it is also an excellent spot in which to view the magnificent sable antelope. Nearby, the S145 branches off to the right. This route is open only to visitors staying at *Talamati Bush Camp.* Some years ago, I spent several weeks at Talamati and experienced excellent viewing and photography. There are plenty of lion in the area, and cheetah are also seen quite regularly.

Although Satara is noted for its frequency of lion sightings, there is also a good chance of seeing cheetah in this area.

The Delagoa thorn, a typical bushveld acacia tree, is common to the west of Satara.

The **Fairfield water hole** is situated in close proximity to the camp, and offers good afternoon photography for large zebra herds and giraffe. As with all the bush camps, Talamati offers peace and exclusivity during holiday periods, when many of the Kruger Park's camps are crowded.

A further seven kilometres south on the S36 lies the **Ngwenyeni Dam**. The dam attracts good numbers of waterbuck, along with other game. From here, I prefer to backtrack a little and explore the S125 **N'waswitsontso Loop**. This attractive 20-kilometre route closely follows

The spectacular blood lily blooms soon after the first summer rains.

the river course. Lion are often present along this road, as well as giraffe and sometimes elephant.

At the end of this road, which joins the main H1-3 Satara–Skukuza route, I recommend driving south for six kilometres and branching off onto the S86. The S86 is only a short loop of four kilometres, and is often overlooked by visitors. I have had excellent sightings here and have seen lion on just about every occasion I have driven this route. If you use the main H1-3 to return to Satara, be sure to stop off at **Nkaya Pan**. Leopard are sometimes seen drinking at this pan.

I sometimes feel the Park's authorities have made viewing terribly easy for visitors at Satara, as many of the best routes have been tarred. A prime example is the H7 main tar road leading to Orpen. Although very busy with traffic, game is prolific. Heading west from Satara, the first few kilometres traverse open plains that abound with zebra and wildebeest, and very often, lion. Surprisingly – because such open habitat is not usually ideal for an animal that prefers to hunt under thick cover – even leopard are seen here.

After travelling for about seven kilometres along the H7, you will reach the **Nsemani Dam** – a very popular location, where visitors often park on the road where it crosses the dam wall. The view from here is far too distant for good photography, but game- and bird-watching with binoculars is rewarding. Even if big game is absent, there is always plenty to see. On my last trip to Kruger, a frog migration took place around this dam, and at least 20 hamerkop as well as a pair of rare and endangered saddle-billed stork enjoyed the feast.

From Nsemani Dam, I advise you to take the short, circular drive on the S40 and S12 roads that branch off of the H7. Here **Girivana water hole** and the surrounding region are noted for regular lion sightings, as well as a host of other game. After rejoining the H7, this road traverses some interesting and very productive game areas. I have frequently encountered leopard while driving along this route – both in the early and later hours of the day. These magnificent cats seem to have become accustomed to the regular, heavy traffic here, and they are quite relaxed and easy to photograph. As you approach Orpen, there is a good chance of spotting cheetah.

The small but rather pleasant camp at Orpen comprises only a dozen or so huts. There are no camping facilities. Campers are accommodated at nearby *Maroela*, and additional accommodation is available in the form of permanent tents at *Tamboti*.

A pair of adult giraffe cautiously approach the Fairfield water hole near Talamati Bushveld Camp. These, the tallest animals in the world, will splay their front legs and lower their heads to the level of the water in order to drink.

The camp site at Maroela is particularly attractive, and is generally quiet and peaceful during the week, but can be noisy at weekends, as large groups of people often visit from the nearby town of Phalaborwa.

Heading back to Satara, I would recommend that you take the detour via **Rabelais Dam** on the S106. I have seen big herds of game drinking here in the mid-morning; unfortunately, though, this highly productive water hole is a little too distant for good photography.

An alternative return route to Satara would be to take the rather long detour through to **Timbavati picnic site** on the S39. **Leeubron water hole**, on the way, is often packed with a good deal of game, but other than that, this road offers sparse viewing opportunities.

From Timbavati, it is a short drive along the S127 to join the main H1-4 tar road leading back to Satara. The H1-4 crosses flat country, and although the scenery may be a little drab, excellent numbers of game may be seen along this road.

Depending on conditions, large herds of elephant and buffalo are to be found along the H1-4, as are the 'plains game' such as zebra and wildebeest.

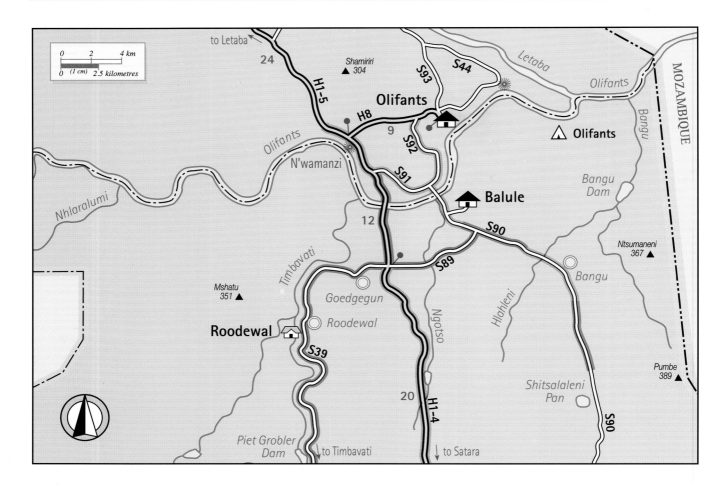

This very large camp is perched atop a steep cliff, and offers wonderful panoramic views of the Olifants River valley. Many birds of prey soar on updrafts created by the elevated location, and with the naked eye one can see hippo wallowing in the river, and other game drinking at the banks. Through binoculars, many other game species can be seen on the apparently endless plains that stretch from the other side of the river. The gardens and rockeries within the camp are filled with indigenous trees and shrubs, notably aloe species. The surrounding area comprises varied habitat, with access to the central plains in the south and outstanding river drives close to camp, while the northern region marks the transition to mopane veld.

One of my favourite drives from Olifants is it to take the H8 heading west, and take a left turn onto the S92 river route. This very productive road warrants slow and thorough investigation. Herds of buffalo and elephant are often present, as well as plenty of giraffe, and unusually high numbers of waterbuck. The fairly open country also makes the S92 a prime route for photographers. The road follows the **Olifants River** for most of its seven kilometres and then splits into the S90 and S91.

Twelve kilometres to the south of Olifants is a small, rustic camp called *Balule*. Accommodation here comprises a mere six huts and 10 camp sites, providing a rather pleasant, intimate atmosphere. A big baobab grows in a corner of the camp, and hyena regularly patrol the fenceline at night. Situated as it is right in the middle of the best game area in the region, Balule is a good choice for the bush enthusiast seeking good viewing in quiet surroundings.

Leading south, the S90 first crosses the river. This low-level bridge is a fine spot to stop for a few minutes to observe the rare white-crowned plovers that rest on the sandbanks. From time to time, I have also had outstanding opportunities to photograph elephant from this bridge. Very good viewing is likely along the S90 up to and sometimes a little beyond **Bangu water hole**. In the dry season, Bangu

Hippopotamus and crocodile may be observed from the high-level bridge spanning the Olifants River on the main H1-4 road. Numbers of both of these animals are substantial in the Park.

is a great magnet for sizeable herds of zebra and wildebeest. The animals tend to loiter in this area, even after drinking, so huge numbers may accumulate. When there are no zebra or wildebeest present it is very likely that lion are in the vicinity, so it is worthwhile to scan the surrounding area. The S90 continues for a considerable distance into the Satara region, but I have not had much luck on this section of the route, and so recommend backtracking to join the S91. This five-kilometre road is another of Olifant's prime routes. So much can be seen along this road that I often wish it were much longer! Giraffe here are very relaxed and easy to photograph, and lion and hyena sightings are common on this road. All too soon, the S91 joins the main H1-4 tar road.

For the next six kilometres to the north, the H1-4 road closely follows the Olifants River, with superb views. Some interesting but short tracks leading off the main road allow a closer look at the river. Lion are regularly spotted here, and the presence of large baboon troops can almost be guaranteed. Although much of the Olifants region appears to be ideal leopard country, sightings of this spotted cat

A spotted hyena makes a nocturnal patrol along the perimeter fence at Balule Camp.

The many rocky outcrops near Olifants are home to the klipspringer.

are inexplicably rather rare, and my only leopard sighting in the region was made on this road.

Another optional route is to head south on the H1-4, crossing the wide but shallow Olifants at the high-level bridge. Bird-watchers with powerful binoculars will be well rewarded, and may, if they are extremely lucky, spot the Pel's fishing owl, which an excited bird enthusiast told me he had seen here.

Follow the H1-4 for another four kilometres until you reach the crossroads where the S89 and S39 join the H1-4. Slow down and keep a lookout for the hyena clan that regularly uses the roadside culvert at this point as a breeding den.

From here, the S89 warrants quick exploration, as both cheetah and wild dog are sighted quite regularly. However, S39 leading west and south along the **Timbavati River** is probably a more interesting option. From **Goedgegun water hole** this becomes a very pretty route with fair numbers of game.

Look out for an unsignposted narrow track on the right. The track does not appear to lead anywhere at first, but after a while a magnificent pool appears, overlooked by a sheer cliff. To date I have seen only waterbuck drink here, although judging by spoor in the parking area,

A 'secret' water hole is to be found on an unmarked track leading off the S39 gravel road.

Burchell's or plains zebra gather in great numbers at Bangu water hole during the dry winter months. Zebras live in large family groups, consisting of a stallion and his mares, and their offspring.

elephant and rhino utilise the pool regularly as well. Continuing south on the S39, herds of zebra, wildebeest and impala are often present at the open, heavily grazed area in the vicinity of **Roodewal water hole**. After passing the turnoff to *Roodewal Private Camp*, some fine herds of kudu may be seen, and leopard sightings are often reported from this area. Further along, you will reach the **Piet Grobler Dam**. This is a large area of water and there appear to be a few places where concentrations of game drink. Hippo are present in the dam, and a recently constructed hide is well situated in order to appreciate this view.

To the north of Olifants, there is a dramatic change of habitat to the mopane veld of the far north. The S44 is an attractive road that can be reached by taking a right turn a few kilometres from camp. This scenic route follows the Olifants, and later the **Letaba River**. Generally speaking, river routes throughout Kruger are productive, but apart from a few kudu, waterbuck and the odd lion, I have found game to be sparse along this road. Visitors with limited time at Olifants would do better to concentrate on the drives in the southern areas.

Along the S39 route, rocky rhyolite ridges add variety to the bushveld-dominated landscape.

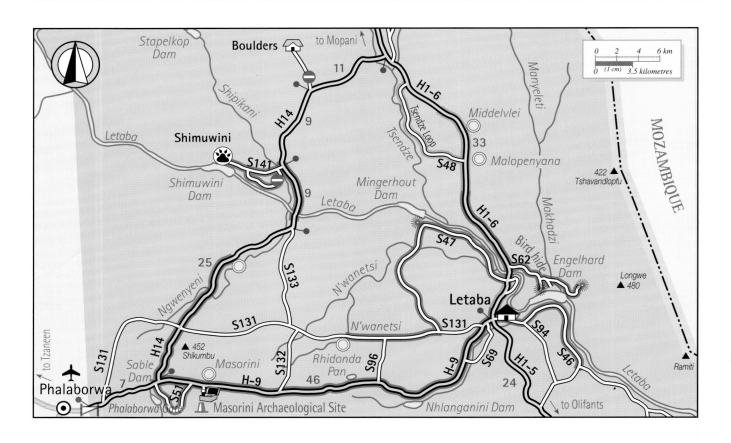

Good numbers of the bateleur eagle occur throughout the Park.

The name Letaba means 'river of sand', which is certainly fitting as the camp overlooks a wide expanse of dry riverbed in the Letaba valley. For much of the year, only small pools remain in the river, but these attract good numbers of game, which can be viewed through binoculars from the restaurant area in the camp. The camp itself is well shaded by some fine specimens of Natal mahogany and apple-leaf. Bird-watching is rewarding, with brown-headed parrot, black-headed oriole and good numbers of mourning doves flitting around the camp.

Although Letaba is a large camp there is seldom a feeling of overcrowding, as traffic spreads out over the many viewing roads in the region. While game is perhaps not as prolific as in some of the prime areas in the south of the Park, Letaba offers a good variety of species, as well as an interesting selection of drives.

Situated a few kilometres to the east of camp, the **Engelhard Dam** is an easily accessible game hot spot. The south bank of the dam can be reached by following the S94 and turning left onto the S46. Although views

A fine buffalo herd crosses the wide, sandy riverbed close to Letaba Camp. Buffalo are heavily built animals, resembling oxen in stature and appearance. Both females and males carry horns, although the male carries the larger set.

are usually too distant for photography, this is a good spot to view game through binoculars. There are many hippo present in the dam, as well as some huge crocodile. Buffalo and elephant herds sometimes amble down to the dam to slake their thirst. Water birds occur here in great numbers and variety. A thorough search should reveal goliath, purple, grey, squacco and green-backed heron, as well as stork, snipe, jacana and black crake.

It is worth following the S46 for some distance past the dam. I have seen lion along this route from time to time, and giraffe and kudu too are quite common in the area. Engelhard Dam can also be reached from the north by heading towards **Mopani Camp** on the H1-6, and taking a right turn to join the S62.

Two interesting, though short side roads offer access to various parts of the dam, and at the end of the S62 there is a splendid **viewpoint.**

It is difficult to decide which of the many viewing routes that radiate from Letaba to follow. I have found the S48 Tsendze Loop to be consistently productive; this road is reached via the H1-6 heading north.

If you take the H1-6 northwards from Letaba, the road follows the **Letaba River**. Big herds of buffalo often cross this vast, sandy riverbed, and giraffe and zebra are usually present here too.

The H1-6 crosses the Letaba River over a high-level bridge and heads due north through mopane country. Lion and cheetah are often seen along the route, and following the first summer rains, kori bustard favour the short grass plains as an arena for their courtship displays. A dozen kilometres along this route and on a short track on the right-hand side, lies **Malopenyana water hole**. Huge herds of buffalo occasionally drink here.

The S48 Tsendze Loop branches off from here to the left. This 17-kilometre gravel road sees little traffic, but offers prolific game when pools of water remain in the **Tsendze River**. When conditions are right, I rate this as the best road in the area.

From here, return to camp via the main H1-6; just to the left lies the busy **Middelvlei water hole**, where impressive herds of zebra and wildebeest gather. Lion also favour the area.

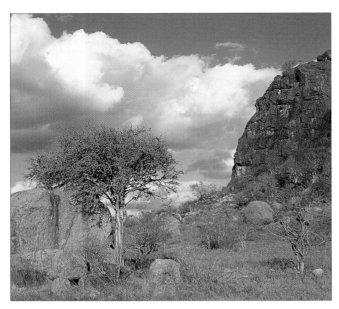

Large koppies *dominate the landscape in the Phalaborwa Gate area.*

Other worthwhile routes in the Letaba region are the S47 and S131 gravel roads, and the H9 and H14 tar routes. The S47 skirts **Mingerhout Dam**, where elephant and buffalo drink. There is a fair chance of spotting lion along the 28-kilometre long S47, and the S131 leading to **N'wanetsi water hole** also warrants investigation.

The H9, leading to **Phalaborwa Gate**, offers a long drive on easy tar road. This route is best avoided at weekends as it carries a lot of local traffic from nearby Phalaborwa. Although it is unusual to see big numbers of game, covering such a lot of ground guarantees a few rewarding sightings. A short distance beyond the **Masorini Archaeological Site**, the short S51 loop, which passes **Sable Dam**, is a worthwhile diversion. The final seven kilometres of the H9 before the gate has little to offer, and if you wish to explore further, the northerly H14 route is a better option.

An old male hippo has a pool all to himself on the Tsendze River north of Letaba.

Shimuwini Bushveld Camp and *Boulders Private Camp* are situated in remote country in the far northwestern reaches of the region. I have sometimes heard visitors pass comment that there is not much game in this area.

Although I have to admit that I have experienced some rather slow days with very few productive times at Shimuwini, the inaccessibility of this camp is attractive. Both camps are far from any of the main camps or entrance gates, which means that only visitors staying at these camps will be on the roads early and late in the day. I have had some of my best opportunities for lion photography in this region, as well as wonderful sightings of cheetah, wild dog and elephant. On top of this, hours would pass before another car arrived at the sighting – not something that is likely to happen in the hustle and bustle in the southern part of the Park!

Many of the smaller spruits only flow briefly after heavy rain.

A majestic male lion photographed alongside the dam barely a kilometre from Shimuwini Bushveld Camp.

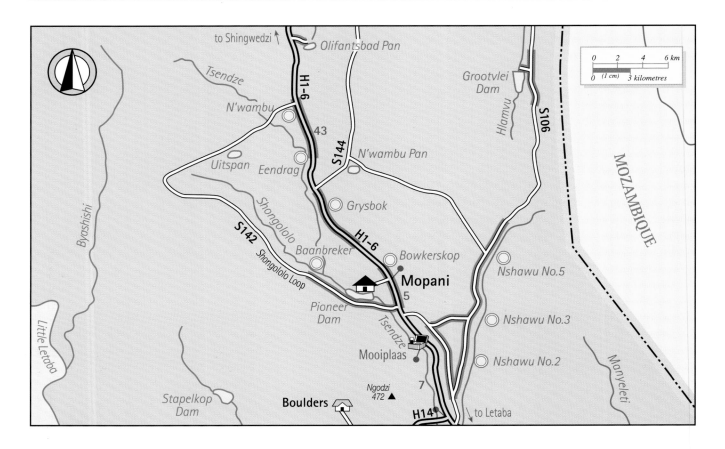

Habituated crested barbet at Mopani Camp.

Set among huge and ancient baobabs in rocky terrain, Mopani offers a magnificent view over **Pioneer Dam**. Elephant drink at the dam in good numbers, allowing visitors to enjoy some fine game-viewing without even having to leave the camp.

In common with much of the shrub-mopane of northern Kruger, game density is rather low in this region. However game-viewing can be productive in late winter, when concentrations of animals build around remaining water sources.

In order to ensure successful game-viewing in the northern part of the Park, it is essential to identify and concentrate on the hot spot areas.

Close to camp, the S142 Shongololo Loop (to the south of Pioneer Dam) usually produces sightings of elephant and other, more commonly seen game species, but it is really only worth driving as far as the **Baanbreker water hole**. At this point, I would change track; even though the S142 continues for another 40 dusty kilometres, on the few occasions I have driven the entire route, I have seen almost nothing along the rest of this road.

An alternative and rather more productive option is to head north on the main H1-6 tar road. The first few kilometres up to **Bowerskop water hole** usually turn up a fair variety of game, and an added bonus is the possibility of spotting the regal sable. Continuing north, sightings are generally rather sparse, but en route, **Grysbok, Eendrag** and **N'wambu water holes** should all have fair numbers of animals drinking by mid-morning.

A further six kilometres along this road, a signpost indicates the turnoff to **Olifantsbad Pan** (Elephant's Bath Pan). To my mind, this is the best water hole in the region for photography, as the access road is ideally situated to allow close views of animals drinking. Paradoxically, I must admit I have yet to see elephant drink here, although spoor in the vicinity confirms that they are regular visitors. Generally the most prolific game in the Mopani region is to be found along the S106 to the east of the camp.

Three water holes, named **Nshawu** and numbered **2, 3** and **5**, lie along this route. These water holes are favoured by elephant, waterbuck, and, occasionally, lion. Some maps still indicate Nshawu Dam between water holes 3 and 5, but unfortunately the dam wall was washed away during recent severe floods. Still on the S106 north, past Nshawu 5, game becomes scarce, and it is only after another 18 kilometres, in the area surrounding Grootvlei Dam, that viewing improves again.

As game-viewing can at times be a little slow in the Mopani region, it is advisable to take longer, exploratory drives in other areas.

Personally, I would suggest a trip to the excellent S48 Tsendze Loop described in the Letaba section, or heading north into the Shingwedzi area. Here I would recommend the very pretty Redrocks route, or, time permitting, going as far as the Kanniedood Dam to the east of Shingwedzi. Although this is a fair trek from Mopani Camp and will take several hours, it should prove worthwhile, as the big elephant and buffalo herds drink at Kanniedood mostly from mid-morning to mid-afternoon.

The Kruger National Park is one of the few remaning strongholds of the highly endangered wild dog. Currently just under 400 of these beautiful 'painted wolves' are resident in the Park.

SHINGWEDZI

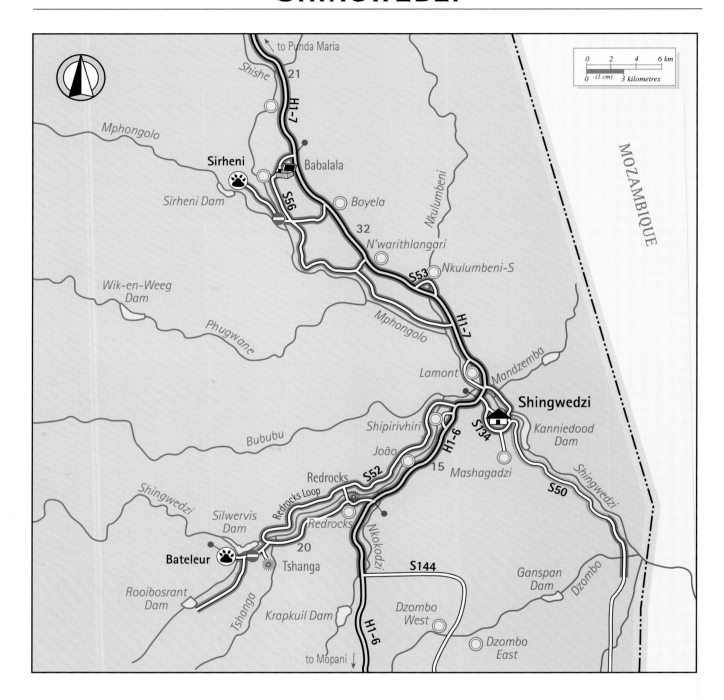

Shingwedzi undoubtedly offers the most productive game-viewing in the northern reaches of the Park. In fact, when conditions are right at the end of the dry season, and **Kanniedood Dam** and the rivers in the area are still holding some water, sightings can be outstanding. I rate Shingwedzi, along with Satara, Lower Sabie, Crocodile Bridge, and Skukuza, as one of the prime game-viewing camps of the Kruger Park.

This medium-sized camp is spacious in layout, so there is seldom a feeling of being overcrowded. The attractive rockeries within the camp have been planted with indigenous aloes and impala lilies, which splash the gardens with a vibrant profusion of colour in the winter season. Keen photographers should keep an eye out for the red-headed weavers that nest near the restaurant, and at several other spots in the camp.

Game drives in the area include some scenic river routes frequented by fine herds of elephant and buffalo. Lion are fairly plentiful in the region, and leopard sightings around Shingwedzi are good.

By far the most popular route close to Shingwedzi is the excellent S50 that closely follows Kanniedood Dam and the **Shingwedzi River**. I believe this to be one of the very best drives in Kruger, both in terms of numbers of game as well as the marvellous scenic views of the river, which is bordered by enormous sycamore figs.

The best section of this route begins only a kilometre or so from camp. Numerous loop roads offer a variety of views of the dam, which holds good numbers of hippopotamus, and many very large crocodile. This is a favoured location of water birds, particularly the endangered saddle-billed stork.

A hide has been built on the dam, but is rather poorly situated and unfortunately offers little advantage for photographers; fortunately, the loop roads generally provide closer views.

Kanniedood Dam is regularly visited by big herds of buffalo and elephant, and these herds frequently remain in the area for a while after drinking.

Beyond the dam, the S50 follows the river course for a considerable distance, and the route continues to be very productive.

The entire road is prime leopard country, and lion are often present as well. The only drawback of this route is its great popularity; the road can become rather dusty during peak periods.

Another fine drive that sees less traffic is the S56 Mphongolo River route. First travel north on the H1-7 main tarred road. It is worth stopping for a moment at **Lamont water hole** along the way as, occasionally, fair numbers of game drink here.

After about five kilometres, you will reach the S56 turnoff. This is another splendid route with impressive old sycamore figs growing along the river bank.

Bird-watching can be particularly rewarding, and a marvellous variety of species will reveal themselves

With the midday temperature approaching 40 °C, an elephant finds relief at the Kanniedood Dam.

Chacma baboon are great fun to watch, and provide endless opportunities for photography.

to the patient observer. Neither will big-game enthusiasts be disappointed, as this represents prime habitat for both lion and elephant.

Approximately 16 kilometres into this route is a large river pool. This is an excellent place to photograph elephant as they slake their thirst. I like to take my time along this road and rarely reach **Babalala picnic site**, which marks the end of the S56, before late morning. Look out for herds of game drinking at **Boyela** and **N'warithlangari water holes** as you return to camp along the H1-7.

Near **Nkulumbeni-S water hole** there is a promising, albeit short detour on the S53. Although I have yet to see much here other than giraffe, it looks to be just the kind of place that could offer interesting sightings.

The S52 Redrocks route is situated to the west of Shingwedzi Camp, and is a personal favourite. Game numbers are perhaps not as great as the Kanniedood Dam drive, but I find the area quite fascinating, and must have driven this road at least 50 times over the years. Rather a long road, the S52 follows the northern bank of the **Shingwedzi River** and then loops back on itself along the southern bank. Both sections are good, but generally I have found the northern section slightly better, so I tend

Visitors are permitted to alight from their vehicles at the Redrocks viewpoint. With a little luck, elephant may be seen drinking at the pool.

The rare and endangered saddle-billed stork is a frequent visitor to Kanniedood Dam.

to drive this first. Leopard have been seen here with remarkable regularity in recent years, and I have seen some fine lion here as well. The road is also notable as one of the most likely places in the Park to see the rare Sharpe's grysbok. The hot spot for these shy antelope lies on the northern side of the loop, just past the turnoff to the causeway river crossing. Elephant herds are sometimes present, but appear to live mostly in areas well away from the tourist routes as they are unused to vehicles. The elephants I have encountered here have behaved skittishly, and even on occasion, with considerable aggression, so it is wise to drive slowly and carefully.

The best **viewpoint** in this region lies on a short loop on the southern side of the river, overlooking **Redrocks water hole**. With a little luck, elephant may be seen drinking at the river pool here.

There are two very fine bushveld camps within the Shingwedzi region. *Bateleur* lies to the west of the Redrocks route, and has a fascinating network of roads accessible only to visitors staying at this bushveld camp. **Rooibosrant** and **Silwervis dams** are close to the camp.

Rooibosrant is a large, shallow dam with big patches of water lilies, making it a prime spot to observe aquatic birds. Good concentrations of game gather here to drink, and on several occasions I have seen lion hunting in the area. It was also at Rooibosrant Dam that I missed a photo opportunity of a lifetime. I was intently photographing a warthog as it drank, when a lioness erupted from the dense mopane and chased its prey around right in front of me. I think I was just as surprised as the warthog, and in the ensuing commotion I botched up the opportunity and recorded nothing at all on film!

Thirty-six kilometres northwest of Shingwedzi is the attractive *Sirheni* camp. Although the six kilometres of road set aside for exclusive use of the camp guests is not especially productive, the **Sirheni Dam** provides good viewing from the camp perimeter fence.

While staying at Sirheni, I have had excellent sightings along the Mphongolo River route; a great advantage of being based at Sirheni is that access to this route is possible long before folks staying at Shingwedzi can reach the area.

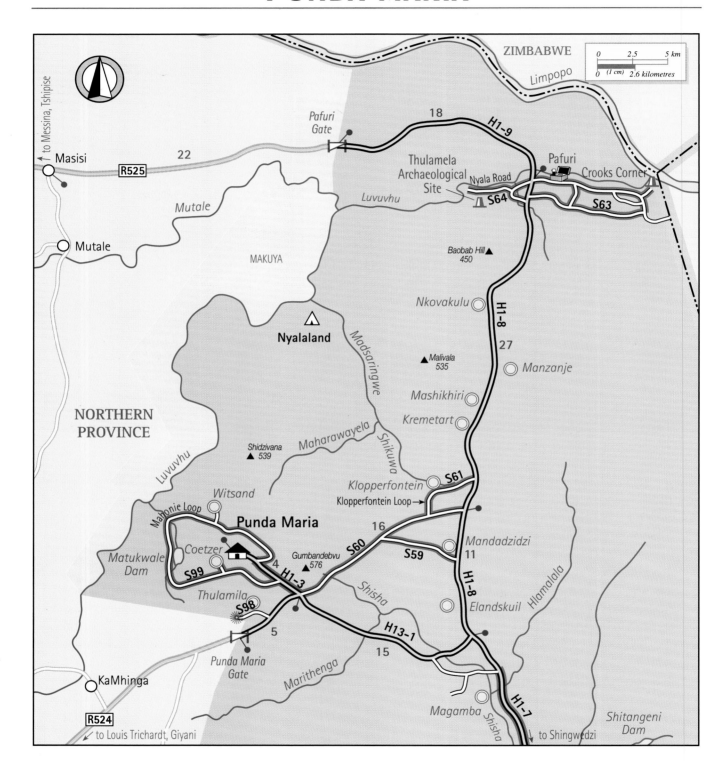

P unda Maria is the northernmost camp in Kruger, and offers interesting drives and easy access to the outstanding Pafuri area. Bird-watchers have a good chance of ticking South African rarities such as thick-billed cuckoo, racket-tailed roller, and a 'special' of mopane habitat, Arnot's chat. A flock of crested guineafowl frequent the camp site, and civet may be seen patrolling along the boundary fence at night. Compared

Crested guineafowl are a forest-dwelling species often encountered in the far north of Kruger.

The wailing call of the trumpeter hornbill is characteristic of the Pafuri region.

to the busy south there is little tourist traffic in this area, making game-viewing a pleasure.

The 26-kilometre S99 Mahonie Loop traces a wide circle around the camp. Although I rate this as one of the best drives in the area, it tends to be rather inconsistent. I hasten to add, though, that I have had wonderful sightings of lion and wild dog on the loop, and kudu and nyala are usually around; Sharpe's grysbok too, may be seen – with a bit of luck! The rare suni is thought to exist in small numbers in the rocky, well-wooded terrain, but I have yet to obtain even a glimpse of this secretive creature.

It is my contention that no one has seen the 'real' Kruger until they have visited Pafuri. There is much to enjoy at Pafuri aside from game: the forest is magnificent, with huge sausage, leadwood, and jackal-berry trees lining the road. Bird life is especially prolific, including Narina trogon, gorgeous bushshrike and trumpeter hornbill. Pel's fishing owl – despite its size, an infuriatingly difficult bird to spot – is also present in this area.

A trip from Punda Maria, the closest camp to Pafuri, still warrants a full day. If you leave camp very early, the first section of the route – the S60 – can yield nyala, kudu, buffalo and elephant sightings. It is a good idea to take a steady, slow drive along this road, as elephant have the unnerving habit of suddenly materialising out of the dense mopane! I recommend taking the short S61 detour – mainly to take a look at the huge baobab that grows very close to the road just past the **Klopperfontein water hole**.

Once on the H1-8 main road I find it best to pick up a bit of speed in order to reach Pafuri as early as possible. There is usually very little game to be seen along this road, although the famous baobab at **Baobab Hill** must be the most photographed tree in the entire Park. From here the road drops away towards the Luvuvhu valley. There is a striking change in vegetation as the rather monotonous mopane veld is replaced by towering green riverine forest.

When you reach Pafuri, I recommend a trip along the western S64, appropriately named Nyala road – not only for the animal but also for the tree. Ancient baobabs grow along this scenically spectacular route. While game is not plentiful, bushbuck, waterbuck and impala are fairly common. Guided walks to the fabulous **Thulamela Archaeological Site** leave from Nyala road; however, it is best to prebook a place on the tour.

The road bridge over the **Luvuvhu River** offers a rewarding view, particularly for bird enthusiasts, as both mottled and Böhm's spinetails are regularly seen here, along with African finfoot and white-crowned plover. The S63 loop leading to **Crooks Corner** yields kudu, nyala, buffalo and lion, and I have heard reports of bushpig sightings in the undergrowth here. The Luvuvhu River is home to a good hippo population, and short river loops allow good views of these animals.

Guided walks are conducted to view the Thulamela Archaeological Site.

PHOTO TIPS

The Kruger National Park presents some unique opportunties as well as considerable difficulties for the wildlife photographer. On the plus side, most animal species, as well as many birds, are exceptionally habituated to the presence of vehicles. Many species that are shy and almost impossible to photograph in other reserves, will hardly bother to glance up when you stop to watch them from the Kruger roads. The great diversity of wildlife also offers a wealth of photo opportunities.

One of the greatest difficulties is that, unlike some of the East African reserves, off-road driving is strictly prohibited. Often subjects are simply too far away or in a bad position for photography. Added to this, thick bush, and at times very long grass, can make a clear view impossible. Also the sheer number of vehicles present – particularly when lion are sighted – can make it awkward to get into exactly the right spot for a good picture. Having said that, it is possible to take some great wildlife photographs in Kruger – all that is required is a little patience and perseverance.
I hope the following hints and tips will add to your enjoyment and enhance the quality of your photography when in the Park.

LIGHTS ...

GOOD LIGHT is essential for good photography. The first two hours of sunlight after dawn, and the two hours before sunset offer soft, golden light that will make your pictures positively 'glow'.

ON AN OVERCAST DAY, the reverse applies. Best times are between mid-morning and mid-afternoon – when the light is brightest. Fortunately, in cool, overcast conditions, animal activity usually continues right through the day.

ON DULL DAYS, adding a little flash to the natural light can greatly enhance an image. Fill-flash is quite a tricky technique to master, so read your camera instruction manual thoroughly before you visit the Park!

ONLY A HANDFUL OF WATER HOLES are well positioned to take good pictures of individual animals drinking. Although most water holes are too distant, worthwhile images can still be taken of big herds trekking to and fro.

CAMERA ...

KEEP A CAMERA FITTED with flash and a 70-200mm zoom handy when back at camp in the evening. Genet often prowl around in the camps looking for braai scraps, and hyena and civet regularly patrol the perimeter fences.

WHEN USING TELEPHOTO LENSES, a steady, firm camera support is essential to take sharp pictures. Use either a bean bag or a camera bracket designed for use in a vehicle to keep your camera steady.

BEFORE TAKING PHOTOGRAPHS, turn off the engine of your vehicle, as vibrations from the motor, even when idling, will cause your pictures to blur.

NO MATTER WHETHER SHOOTING PRINTS OR SLIDES, 100ASA film is a good all-round choice for the Kruger Park. It is worth carrying a couple of rolls of fast 400ASA film as well, for very dull conditions, or to get extra reach for flash photography at night.

When exploring the park, it pays to drive slowly, as hyenas often sit or lie only metres from the roadside.

ACTION ...

WHEN YOU SPOT A GOOD SUBJECT, don't just snap a few pictures and move on. As long as the animal stays within range, hang in there. Sooner or later something interesting *will* happen.

FOR MANY VISITORS, spotting and photographing the Big Five is a priority. However, the common antelope species can also make great pictures. Even impala, especially when accompanied by oxpeckers, can make a fascinating study.

SIMILARLY, CHACMA BABOON and vervet monkey are wonderful photo subjects. Interaction within the troop, and particularly youngsters at play, provide such a wealth of opportunities that you may run out of film!

THE BEST AND EASIEST bird photography can be done in the rest camps. The birds here are so used to human activity that a modest tele-lens is all that is necessary to take excellent portraits.

WILDLIFE DOCUMENTARIES (and, I have to admit, probably wildlife books as well!) that are usually the result of months or sometimes years of work, can create unrealistic expectations for the visitor. Have fun photographing the more commonly seen subjects. Look on it as a bonus if you get really lucky and photograph a lion chase and kill, or a magnificent leopard on the hunt.

CHECKLIST

aardvark .... ☐
aardwolf .... ☐

baboon, chacma .... ☐
badger, honey .... ☐
buffalo, Cape .... ☐
bushbaby, lesser .... ☐
    greater/thick-tailed .... ☐
bushpig .... ☐

caracal .... ☐
cat, African wild .... ☐
cheetah .... ☐
civet .... ☐

dassie .... ☐
duiker, common/grey .... ☐
    red .... ☐

eland .... ☐
elephant .... ☐

fox, bat-eared .... ☐

genet, large-spotted .... ☐
giraffe .... ☐
grysbok, Sharpe's .... ☐

hare, Cape .... ☐
    scrub .... ☐
hartebeest, Lichtenstein .... ☐
hippopotamus .... ☐
hyena, spotted .... ☐

impala .... ☐

jackal, black-backed .... ☐
    side-striped .... ☐

klipspringer .... ☐
kudu .... ☐

leopard .... ☐
lion .... ☐

mongoose, banded .... ☐
    dwarf .... ☐
    slender .... ☐
    white-tailed .... ☐
monkey, vervet .... ☐

nyala .... ☐

oribi .... ☐
otter, Cape clawless .... ☐

pangolin .... ☐
porcupine .... ☐

reedbuck, common .... ☐
    mountain .... ☐
rhebok, grey .... ☐
rhinoceros, black .... ☐
    white .... ☐
roan .... ☐

sable .... ☐
serval .... ☐
springhare .... ☐
squirrel, tree/mopane .... ☐
steenbok .... ☐
suni .... ☐

tsessebe .... ☐

warthog .... ☐
waterbuck .... ☐
wild dog .... ☐
wildebeest, blue .... ☐

zebra, Burchell's .... ☐